BURLINGTON

BURLINGTON

Photographs by John de Visser
Text by Jane Irwin

Stoddart

A BOSTON MILLS PRESS BOOK

Canadian Cataloguing in Publication Data

De Visser, John, 1930–
   Burlington

ISBN 1-55046-127-3

1. Burlington (Ont.) - Pictorial works.
2. Burlington (Ont.) - History - Pictorial works.
I. Irwin, Jane, 1941–   . II. Title.

FC3099.B8D48 1995   971.3'533   C95-930752-4
F1059.5.B8D48 1995

First published in 1995 by
Stoddart Publishing Co. Ltd.
34 Lesmill Road
Toronto, Canada
M3B 2T6
(416) 445-3333

A BOSTON MILLS PRESS BOOK
The Boston Mills Press
132 Main Street
Erin, Ontario
N0B 1T0

Edited by Kathleen Fraser
Designed by Mary Firth
Printed in Canada

The publisher gratefully acknowledges the support of the
Canada Council, Ontario Ministry of Culture and
Communications, Ontario Arts Council and Ontario
Publishing Centre in the development of writing and
publishing in Canada.

*Photographs. Front cover: Joseph Brant House Museum.
Back cover: Mount Nemo. Page 1: An avenue in Roseland.
Page 2: Spencer Smith Park, with the old breakwater wall.
Facing page: The pier by the shipping channel, with the
Toronto skyline like a distant mirage.*

CONTENTS

Above: The renovated waterfront promenade at Spencer Smith Park. Facing page: The garden of the Gingerbread House

ACKNOWLEDGMENTS

Many kind readers of my first draft supplied information, suggestions and corrections. I especially wish to thank Eric Gudgeon for his scrupulous reading and attention to historical details, and Grant and Kathleen Whatmough for their interest and helpful comments. Gar Darroch, Janis Topp and Ian Ross have helped in several ways. If not every error has been caught, the fault is mine.

It has been a great pleasure to work with John de Visser, whose photographs have illuminated so many admirable publications, and with John Denison, publisher of Boston Mills Press, whose enthusiastic endorsement of the Burlington book project has made it happen. Designer Mary Firth and editors Noel Hudson and Kathleen Fraser have brought their professional skills and patience to the task, and I have enjoyed working with them.

Richard Bachmann may not be "the onlie begetter" of this book; but without him it, and many other good things besides, would not have come to be. My part of the book is dedicated to him.

A Burlington sunrise

INTRODUCTION

The city of Burlington, Ontario, has a special character formed by two natural features of world renown—the Niagara Escarpment and Lake Ontario. The city's southern boundary is created by the waterfront of the lake itself, the large bay at the head of the lake, and the sand strip reaching out between them. North of the bay, Burlington's northern boundary follows the face of the Escarpment. From there, it runs northward along the Halton–Flamborough boundary line to Derry Road, some 12 miles (19 km) or so north of the lakeshore; then east along the Derry Road, passing just south of the great Escarpment promontory known as Rattlesnake Point. The eastern border then runs south along Bell School Line, Tremaine Road, and Burloak Drive to the lakeshore again. On a map, Burlington's large area (more than 72 square miles, or 188 km²) is delineated by surveyed straight lines—borders that bulge slightly at the Escarpment but ignore the great cleft of the Bronte Creek valley—and the naturally variable line of the lakeshore.

The Escarpment is recognized by UNESCO as a World Biosphere Reserve. For almost a decade, the Niagara Escarpment Commission has balanced, as on a tightrope, between the need to preserve a valuable ecosystem and the pressure to intensify its development value. Since the public display of high-wire walking above the Niagara Gorge is no longer permitted, the NEC balancing act is occasionally the most thrilling show on the Escarpment.

As part of the St. Lawrence Seaway system, Lake Ontario is an international shipping route. Great tankers under foreign flags constantly pass Burlington en route to

Rural-route postal delivery on Britannia Road

Above: A boutique window in the Village Square
Facing page: A view from Mount Nemo

priority by agencies such as the Waterfront Regeneration Trust. Concrete bunkers are coming down, sandy beaches are opening up. It's easier than ever to dabble our toes in the water.

Burlingtonians are increasingly sensitive to environmental issues. We have in our midst much professional expertise—the Canada Centre for Inland Waters, for instance—but our awareness is also prompted by first-hand amateur experience. We can walk the nature trails of the Royal Botanical Gardens, hike the Bruce Trail, and visit sites conserved for public use by the Halton Region Conservation Authority.

The acronymns so familiar to Burlingtonians—HRCA, NEC, RBG, CCIW, GO Transit, the QEW—represent the experience and the imprint of the people who have lived here. Our natural setting has been shaped and reshaped by human actions. In the seventeenth century, this area was an aboriginal trading centre. In the nineteenth century, settlers and farmers transformed the forest and swampland into "The Garden of Canada," shipping choice fruits to international markets. At the turn of the twentieth century, Burlington was transformed again by the "Lakeshore Surveys" of an especially enlightened developer. W.D. Flatt had a vision of the "suburb beautiful" along the lakeshore. His conception of Craftsman style included the promotion of modern designs, traditional craft skills, sensitivity to the natural environment, and provision for a great variety of recreational activities. He implemented his vision by making substantial investments of the fortune he had made as a young man in the timber export business in Wisconsin. Eighty years later, in a city that has grown and expanded many times over, elements of the Craftsman-style ethos and lifestyle remain strong and vigorous.

Perhaps as a result of the underlying conservative bias of Burlington residents, much of the area is, to a large

the docks of steelworks and refineries in neighbouring cities. Now, after decades of industrial use, the waters of the lake and bay are being reclaimed as a natural habitat, and public access to our great lake is being made a

extent, unspoiled. Despite its location in the midst of one of the biggest and most rapidly developing urban regions in North America, Burlington has retained its special characteristics. In 1958 the Town of Burlington amalgamated with the southern part of East Flamborough and Nelson Township, expanding to its present boundaries to become, overnight, "the biggest town in Canada"; some said, "the biggest small town in Canada." It lost its big-town status when it became a city in 1974, but has kept its extraordinary diversity. The Aldershot and Plains area retains its distinct character, as do the historic villages of Lowville and Kilbride, and even the former hamlet of Zimmerman. The rural lands north of Dundas Street are still being farmed. Driving down country sideroads, passing by rolling acres of

Mallards, Canada geese, and one refugee from a farmyard pond, at Sioux Lookout

fertile farmland, century farms, and grand timber-frame barns, visitors are often heard to ask, "Are we still in Burlington?" Yes, we are.

Then we drive south on Cedar Springs Road to Dundas Street, and see spread below us a panorama of the immense building and development boom of the past thirty years. It was Governor Simcoe who commissioned the survey of Dundas Street, as part of what became known as "the Governor's Road," to serve as a military route, and also to open up land for settlement. Could we imagine ourselves two hundred years ago, alongside the settlers charged with the task of clearing a way through the wilderness? We might still identify and recognize this location. In two hundred years, the contours of the lake, the bay, and the Escarpment have changed—from this vantage point—only imperceptibly.

The skyway, the highways and the highrises, our new territorial markers, show how many of us have come to settle here. Most of us who live in Burlington today are not natives but newcomers. We have arrived, road map in hand, making inquiries of our new neighbours and calling on the services of Information Burlington as we explore our newly adopted home. We have pushed the population total to 133,945 and rising, at last count. Longer-established families have played their part, too. The Walker family, for instance, arrived in 1816 and has lived here for eight generations. Edgar Walker recalled that in 1936 his bride became "the fifth Mrs Walker in less than one mile." In an era when many families are more dispersed, it is good to live in a city that soon makes us feel so much at home.

John de Visser's camera has captured, as you will see for yourselves, the variety and sublime beauty of our natural environment. He also gives us glimpses of the way we live now—the comforts and attractions of civic and community life in Burlington.

Suburban Burlington

The Indian Wells Golf Club, seen from Mount Nemo

CHAPTER ONE

FATHER'S DAY AT HIDDEN LAKE

People who live in Burlington, many of them, work to earn their living. But there's also well-earned retirement, and taking a break, and even combining business with recreation. Hence the dozen or so golf and country clubs within the bounds of Burlington. Their grounds are unusually scenic. Some of the courses were shaped almost entirely by natural forces and only minimally by mechanical earth-movers. Lowville Heights Golf Club, for example, is aptly named. Its natural ups and downs present added challenges to golfers. There the profile of Mount Nemo looks on, unmoved, whether you are over or under par. The Burlington Golf & Country Club, on the North Shore of Burlington Bay, has impressive scenery of another type—the so-called million-dollar view of the Hamilton steel mills, where so many millions have been made.

This summer morning on No. 1 Side Road, avid golfers are taking on the challenges of thirty-six championship holes. It's Father's Day, and dozens of fathers are enjoying their weekend treat, rolling their carts over the course at Hidden Lake Golf & Country Club. The lake is concealed within a dense growth of encircling trees and can only be glimpsed from the seventeenth hole. The path down to the water's edge is not inviting, and the lake itself gives the impression of having something to hide. Its waters are deep and dark. People say it is bottomless. It is rumoured to have the properties of a black hole; anything or anybody that falls into this lake will never be seen again. This sinister reputation is quite unjustified, however. It is simply a spring-fed lake and goes down about 80 feet (24 m). The lower 60 feet (18 m) of these depths are a suspended layer of murky ooze. Like the more famous Walden Pond, it has no visible outlet. Surface water evaporates, mostly invisibly, and some of the deep water seeps slowly into the underlying layers of rock.

This is Lake Medad, so named after a neighbouring settler, Medad Parsons. *His* name was taken from the Old Testament. Perhaps the family Bible was opened at random by his parents or godparents at Numbers 11:26: "And the name of the one was Eldad, and the name of the other Medad." Was there also an Eldad Parsons? If so, we know of no lake named after him.

The soaring dragonflies, the jumping fish, the croaking herons—none of these lively creatures lessens the strong impression that the lake is uninhabited. Somehow, it is not the absence of the Parsons family that is the cause of our unease. It seems to linger from an earlier period. Of course, a so-called Indian legend is attached to this place. Something about a tribe of people who lived long ago in this

land of plenty, in such ease, prosperity and ennui that they turned to murder and mayhem. A son played William Tell with his father, but deceitfully, and reversing the roles. His arrow stopped his father's life. At last this dysfunctional people met their annihilation when they were all swallowed up by the lake in a terrible deluge. The fish leaping in the peaceful waters are the souls of the lost people, and it was said that no Indian would take one of those evil spirits from the lake.

The aboriginal peoples are not here to tell their stories themselves, although they have left many relics. Their tools for living—flint arrowheads, stone tools and calumets, pottery, and shell beads—and their ossuaries, the revered memorials for their dead, have been uncovered over and over again in areas close to Lake Medad. More enduring are their trails. It is not entirely true that—as some newcomer wrote at the beginning of this century— "a hundred years ago this fertile land was a trackless forest, the abode of the Indian and the savage beast." We are still walking in the tracks of our aboriginal predecessors. Or, more probably, driving in their tracks, and not just on the Hidden Lake golf course, but on our major roads. It has been said that Plains Road, Waterdown Road, King Road, and even Snake Road, with a hundred and fifty turns in 5 miles (about 8.5 km), were former trails of the Neutral nation. Most of those trails converged not far from Lake Medad, at the settlement of Kandoucho, the centre of the Neutral economy, which was based on agriculture, hunting, and trading.

In the seventeenth century, the travelling men of New France began to find their way to Kandoucho. First the Jesuit fathers, who reported that "terror had gone before" them and caused "the doors of cabins everywhere to be closed" to them. Some time later the Neutral village disappeared from the eastern shore of the lake. The site has been the subject of much archeological study and interpretation. The trees growing from its abandoned ash-pits have been estimated to be about three hundred years old. Were the Neutrals wiped out by enemy action? They were not entirely neutral, but were involved in occasional armed warfare. Or did they find the infectious diseases of the Europeans, such as smallpox, harder to resist than their religious doctrines?

In the autumn of 1669, at the nearby Neutral settlement of Tinawatawa, an unexpected meeting occurred. The explorer Louis Joliet, on his way back to Québec, met Father René de Brehant de Galinée and Father Dollier de Casson, along with René Robert Cavalier, Sieur de la Salle. What a fine company of patronymics: de Brehant de

Above: The "million-dollar view" by night
Facing page: Golfers

Galinée, de Casson, de la Salle. Men trailing the names of their families and fatherlands through tracts of unnamed territories. In later years, Joliet and La Salle were to explore, separately and successfully, the Mississippi River. La Salle would follow the Mississippi all the way down to its mouth in the Gulf of Mexico. But on this occasion it seems he had no interest in tracing the course of Grindstone Creek. He was only making a short detour after coming ashore at a spot that is now the site of the present-day La Salle Park and Pavilion. But the park and pavilion are part of another story.

Above: Cleaning up downtown Burlington on John Street
Facing page: The Gingerbread House on Ontario Street

The Joseph Brant House Museum

CHAPTER TWO

JOSEPH BRANT AND HIS HOUSE

The end of the pier of the Burlington Canal offers the best view of the shoreline from here to Toronto. Well, Toronto is really just a low haze on the horizon, but we know it is there. Gleaming out from a slightly less hazy mass of downtown bank office towers—apparently floating on the surface of the lake—the CN Tower reflects some beams of solar energy our way. The curve of the shoreline conceals from view the suburbs of Metropolitan Toronto and our lakeshore neighbours, Bronte and Oakville. So, right next to the mirage-like vision of the CN tower, but much closer to us, we see the shoreline of Burlington. First in our line of sight are the wooded shores, behind which shelter the residences of Lakeshore Road; then, beyond the green ribbon of Spencer Smith Park, the great masses of downtown condominiums and apartments, with their grand names: Harbourview, Centennial, Village Square, Upper Canada Place, Grande Regency. These are fine addresses indeed, and their balconies provide marvellous views. But from our standpoint on the pier, the most visible building along the shore—the one that most attracts our eye—is a two-storey frame house whose white paint glows like a beacon in every quality of atmospheric light. In bright sunlight the house dazzles. In twilight and gloaming, it gathers all the ambient light from air and water to itself and reflects it out like a signal.

In 1803 the Brant House was under construction. Cedar logs for the structure were brought from the Thousand Islands, at the other end of Lake Ontario; the narrow clapboard siding was cut from local trees. This was truly a Grand Regency house, built during the regency of the future George IV of England, in an elegant architectural combination of Georgian and Regency styles. The two-storey residence was like those being built in the capital towns of Upper Canada, Newark and York, now Niagara-on-the-Lake and Toronto. At that time, in this area, its only neighbouring buildings were reported to be "a great number of huts." It had a centre-hall plan, with an entrance portico facing the lake. In 1819 the British consul at New York, James Buchanan, approaching along the shore of Lake Ontario, could see the Brant House, "which had a very noble and commanding aspect," from miles away. "Driving up to the door we alighted. The outer door leading into the spacious hall was open; we entered and seeing no person about proceeded into the parlour.... It was a room well-furnished, with a carpet, pier- and

chimney-glasses, mahogany tables, fashionable chairs, a guitar, a neat hanging book-case in which among other volumes we perceived a Church of England Prayer Book translated into the Mohawk tongue...."

Visitors today will see a similar hall and parlour—although they will certainly be met at the door, probably by someone in historical costume. This is now the Joseph Brant House Museum, where we are invited to step back in time to the nineteenth century. Agreeable as the illusion of time travel may be, however, we are reminded here that history is a continuous, on-going process, and not merely something that happened in the past. The Brant House, to an even greater extent than most historical houses, is like our great-grandfather's axe—the handle of which has been replaced once and the axe-head twice. If you are looking for the original fabric of the house, you will be shown a portion of one of the original cedar logs. If you are looking for the original site of the house, you may or may not find it. This house has not just "seen" two centuries of change, as we may say of buildings whose settings have altered beyond recognition. It has undergone a metamorphosis of its own. In that respect it is a suitable last residence for Joseph Brant, originally named Thayendanegea, an enigmatic, intriguing character whose own life crossed cultural and geographical divides.

Burlington shares Joseph Brant with Brantford, a city to the west of us. Land along the Grand River was granted to the Six Nations, who fought for the Loyalist cause during the American Revolutionary War, in compensation for the loss of their ancestral lands in the Mohawk Valley of New York State. Brant was never a hereditary Mohawk chief ("Chief Joseph Brant" is a misnomer). But he was an effective representative of Mohawk interests to the British colonial governors. In 1775, before the outbreak of the Revolutionary War, Brant travelled to London and appeared at court. His portrait by George Romney, commissioned by his friend the Earl of Warwick, still hangs today in the grandeur of eighteenth-century Syon House. After the war was over, Brant returned to be presented to George III and Queen Charlotte, and to become friends with the Duke of Northumberland and the Prince of Wales, the future Prince Regent himself. Brant's social triumphs did not, however, enable him to negotiate land-grant deeds for the Six Nations that were equivalent to the land grants provided for United Empire Loyalists of European origins.

Brant was well aware of the importance of land titles. His role as liaison between his people and the British government led to his being given formal power of attorney to negotiate land sales from the Grand River tract to non-Mohawk settlers. It is perhaps not entirely coincidental that the ratification of those land sales in 1798 occurred at the same time as Brant's somewhat abrupt departure from Brantford and his move to what is now Burlington. Here he received a personal crown grant of 3,450 acres (about 1,400 ha) of land. The oak tree said to have marked one of the boundaries of his holdings is still flourishing not far from King Road. He was the first freehold landholder at the Head of the Lake. (The Mississaugas from whom this parcel of land had been purchased by the Crown did not, after all, hold registered title to the land.) Quite soon, even before Brant died in 1807, parts of Brant's Block were divided and sold to William Chisholm, Nicholas Kerns, Asahel Davis, Thomas Ghent, and Augustus Bates. Descendants of these pioneers are still living in Burlington.

It would be an exaggeration to claim, as people sometimes do, that Joseph Brant was Burlington's first land developer. But the property transactions, losses, and gains that characterized his own career were to be repeated in the fortunes of the house he left to future generations. His descendants kept the house until the mid-nineteenth century, when it was sold to an entrepreneur who envisioned Burlington's potential as a summer resort. The natural advantages of the Brant House location were improved by the addition of resort amenities: a croquet lawn, an ice-cream parlour, a bowling green, a dance hall, and even bathing booths for discreet private swimming in Brant's Pond. The Hamilton & Northwestern Railway line ran right by, and stopped within easy walking distance.

The 1877 *Illustrated Atlas of Halton* shows a double-page illustration of a vastly expanded structure. "The Brant House Burlington, a Beautiful Summer Resort & European Hotel situated on one of the choicest sites overlooking Burlington Bay & Lake Ontario," had three wings, three

The Skyway and lift bridge at dawn

*The Burlington civic crest
at City Hall*

storeys, six front gables, and a thirteen-bay front elevation. Shown nearby is the original house, with Victorian verandahs and wings obscuring the proportions of the small but elegant Georgian mansion.

In 1897 the Hamilton Radial Electric Company line made it even easier to make a refreshing getaway from the summer heat of Hamilton's city streets. By that time, various proprietors had renovated and updated the Brant House, while still proclaiming it a "quiet family resort." It was purchased in 1898 by A.B. Coleman, the Village of Burlington's first great builder and developer. Several of Coleman's fine houses can still be seen nearby, on Nelson Avenue and Ontario Street especially. The house he built for himself, the Gingerbread House, is a much-loved local landmark. Coleman had a vision of a more deluxe, more sophisticated and cosmopolitan international resort hotel. His four-storey brick structure, with a grand three-level verandah and the famous Roof Garden, was built in 1900 next to the Brant House. The Brant Hotel thrived until July 1917, when the government of Canada suddenly expropriated it to serve as a convalescent hospital for soldiers injured in the Great War. Hundreds of guests who had booked for that summer season were notified that their reservations were cancelled. Six years later, the patients were removed to a hospital in Toronto. The vacated Brant Military Hospital never recovered. It was for a time a residential school for the handicapped, then a summer camp for inner-city children. In the thirties there was a proposal to use it as a hostel for unemployed and homeless men, but it had deteriorated too much even for that purpose. Next to the hotel-hospital, the Brant House stood vacant.

The wrecker's ball brought down house and hotel in 1937. Almost before the rubble was cleared away, people began to think that the old Joseph Brant home ought to be rebuilt on its historic site. Thanks to the strong support of the Honourable T.B. McQuesten of Hamilton, a replica of the original house was built on a generous area of parkland. The shoreline had been altered during the hundred and forty years since the house was first built. Brant's Pond had been filled in. But the replicated house stood in its original location, at the Head of the Lake, with a "noble and commanding aspect" over the water. In 1942 it was formally opened as a historic museum. Fifteen years later, Burlington needed a hospital again. Whether the six years' presence of the wounded of the Great War in the Brant Military Hospital established a sort of historic claim to this land—or for other reasons—this location was chosen, and the Joseph Brant Hospital was built next door to the Joseph Brant Museum. For many years they shared the same parking lot. Recently the hospital has needed room to expand. Thus in 1994 the house was lifted up, put on wheels, and moved 100 feet (about 30 m) to a new foundation. It is closer to the lake, and, in truth, it has an even more noble and commanding aspect—and its own parking lot.

Why all this reconstruction and relocation? It almost seems as if Brant's house echoes the displacements of the man himself. He was by birth a Mohawk of the Wolf clan, but raised as a protégé of his sister's Irish husband, Sir William Johnson, and educated at Moor's Indian Charity School in Connecticut, where Reverend Eleazar Wheelock aimed to propagate Christian knowledge and teach English, Hebrew, Greek and Latin. Brant was the translator of the Gospel of Saint Mark into Mohawk ("resist not evil: but whosoever shall smite thee on thy right cheek, turn to him the other also"), but also a warrior on the British side in the Niagara campaign of the Seven Years' War, the Pontiac Wars, and the War of American Independence.

Born in 1743 while his parents were on a hunting expedition near the Cuyahoga River in Ohio, he died in 1807 a landed gentleman.

We have this description of Brant's hospitality at his Grand River house in 1792:

> Tea was on the table when we came in, served up in the handsomest China plate and every other furniture in proportion. After tea was over we were entertained with the music of an elegant hand organ…. Next day dinner was just going on the table in the same elegant style … the servants dressed in their best apparel. Two slaves attended the table, the one in scarlet, the other in coloured clothes with silver buckles in their shoes and every other part of their apparel in proportion.

But after one of his visits to England, Brant wrote in a letter:

> You ask me then, whether civilization is favourable to human happiness…. I was born of Indian parents and lived among those whom you are pleased to call savages; I was since sent to live among the white people…. After all this experience, I am obliged to give my opinion in favour of my own people…. Among us we have no prisons; we have no pompous parade of courts; we have no written laws; and yet judges are as highly revered amongst us as they are with you and their decisions are as much regarded. Daring wickedness is here never suffered to triumph over helpless innocence. The estates of widows and orphans are never devoured by enterprising sharpers….

In this brave new world, the old cultural values of Europe clashed repeatedly with the old cultural values of native-born Americans. The conflict was perhaps almost evenly matched within the character of Joseph Brant, né Thayendanegea.

THE PARISH CHURCH OF

Saint Luke

ANGLICAN CHURCH OF CANADA
DIOCESE OF NIAGARA

RECTOR
THE VENERABLE D. RALPH SPENCE
ARCHDEACON OF TRAFALGAR

ASSISTANT CURATES
REV. JANE E. HUMPHREYS
REV. NANCY L. FITZPATRICK

SUNDAY SERVICES
8:30 A.M. 9:30 A.M. 11:15 A.M.

WEEKDAY SERVICES
WEDNESDAY 10:00 A.M.

FOUNDED 1834

Except thy vehicle
be designated by
St. Luke's
It shall not
transgress herein
Private Parking By-law 71-1983

Burlington Beach

CHAPTER THREE

THE BEACH STRIP

It's a sunny and breezy Sunday morning. A cluster of sailboats out in the middle of the lake skims lightly about, while a long freighter glides through the channel, silently but with businesslike intent, toward its harbour in the bay. The canal, built in 1832 and marked by the old stone lighthouse, bisects the long strip of sand that is the Beach Strip, and now divides it into the Hamilton side and the Burlington side. The road connecting the two sides is broken by the lift bridge, raised now for the freighter. For more than a hundred and twenty years, road traffic yielded the right-of-way to ships passing through. There were times in the 1950s when the queue of waiting cars on this part of the QEW was a mile long. At last, in 1958, the ribbon was cut and the Skyway opened. We in Burlington call it the Burlington Skyway. The Canal Amusement Park rides are long gone, but what do we care? Now we have the thrill of driving over a bridge 4 miles (6.5 km) long and looking down 120 feet (37 km) into the bay. We're going too fast to see everything, and the trip is even more exciting when the warning signs flash *High Winds on Skyway* at us.

Today though, we are riding sedately on our bicycles, along the renovated lakeshore path. Soon even that speed is too much. We park our bikes and proceed on foot along the shore. The waves leave lap-lines on the smooth, wet sand. Small children with small plastic buckets are collecting small bivalve shells. "Look over here, there's hundreds!" A gaggle of Canada geese has adopted a large, white domestic goose. At this early hour, dogs walk their owners on leashes, oblivious of by-law notices advising that they are not welcome.

Bronzed sun-worshippers have claimed their patches of the beach. One man is so thoroughly carpeted with tattoos, he barely has space left for a suntan. On the volleyball court, outlined by a bright yellow cord, players in action emanate the scent of their sunscreen lotions. Other forms of territory are marked, too. The concrete bases of the hydro towers are covered with multicoloured names and peace symbols. The painted graffiti give us no stronger or more obnoxious advice than to Live in Peace. On quieter stretches of the beach, where the overhanging willows shade the beach, we find the wet sand engraved with more temporary declarations: Alana was here, Aaron was here.

A dozen catamarans are parked in their designated area. One couple is preparing to launch theirs. Now the lifeguards come on duty. One of them is practising in the kayak. And yes, there are even a few people in the water.

Northwestern Railway in 1875 and the Radial line in 1897 that led to the residential development of the strip. Summer cottages were built, some of them very grand, as in Muskoka, and some of them merely functional. Although a few were kept as summer homes, most were insulated, heated, added on to, and converted to year-round use. They don't exactly look their age. Some are very spruce, with all modern conveniences. Others look as if they were improvised a few years ago, from parts found at demolition sites—part

But most of us are content just to look at the lake in its smiling mood, watching it flash dimples of light at us. The downtown is crisply outlined in the distance, but we are far from workaday concerns.

This is a public beach, but one of its charms for us, who are a part of the visiting public, is the special character that it has as a private home place, at least for a small number of remaining residents. Their houses and garden spaces are right next to our public spaces. They look out at us walking past, and they seem not to be bothered by our blocking their view of the lake. After all, we are transient day-trippers: here today, gone tomorrow. And mostly fair-weather friends of the beach. They have watched the water for a long time and know its many moods.

People have lived, however transiently, on the Beach Strip since 1798, but it was the coming of the Hamilton &

tree-house, part handmade house in the style of California beaches of the 1970s. The people who live here are individualists, but they follow neighbourhood traditions too. Their houses may be named Venezuela, or Shangri La. They may have a sign in the window that states Beware: Jumping Spiders. Although they don't go in for all the stereotypical suburban copy-cat trends, they are neighbourly and do enjoy some suburban amenities. Barbeques, of course. Decks of all persuasions, sandbagged or sandswept. The garden of A Summerplace surely merits a Civic Rose Award. With so many tubs full of hibiscus, oleander and exotic evergreens, it could almost pass as a garden centre. We admire and walk on, past a festive patio garlanded with coloured lights. In the yard next door is a beach shack made of weathered boards with a thatched roof, apparently held together by an assortment of ancient

Facing page: The Canada Centre for Inland Waters. Above: The lift bridge up for a freighter

Above: Burlington Beach in midwinter
Facing page: Burlington remembers

licence plates from distant states and provinces. And here is an outdoor English pub complete with dart board, lacking only some timbers, a fireplace, and a licence to serve the public on or off the premises.

The Beach Strip has been a lively residential community for a long time now, but it seems it will not last for much longer. The City owns most of the land on which the cottages were built, and has demolished most of the vacant houses and persuaded many householders to sell. For most inhabitants, 1994 was their last summer on the Beach. Some ten or twelve residents have held out and not sold their cottages. Perhaps they hope for a change in the Halton Region's plans before the year 2000. In the twenty-first century this land may become a much larger public park, no doubt with a vitality of its own. But some of us will regret the disappearance of this stubbornly colourful vignette of cottage life.

Above: The La Salle Park marina. Facing page: Set to go fishing

CHAPTER FOUR

THE LA SALLE PARK AND PAVILION

The North Shore Boulevard is one of Burlington's prime locations for residential real estate. The names that appeared on the 1915 and 1919 surveys—Inglehaven and Glenhaven, with their modest British accents—suggest the character of these artfully landscaped estates, where picturesque neo-Tudor houses are tucked away out of sight. Now and then we may catch a glimpse of roof and stucco and tall chimneys before we return our attention to the ups and downs and winding curves and hidden driveways of the Boulevard. On the secluded bayshore side there are private havens and docks that we cannot see. But here and there the City has acquired small "windows to the lake," where we can pull off the road, sit on a bench, and watch the bay.

It is blowy today, and the grey water is broken by hurried whitecaps. At the horizon, grey clouds scud above the grey outline of the Escarpment, which over there, in Hamilton, is called the Mountain. All this monochrome is interrupted by small fluorescent dots in rapid motion—the lime and red sails of sailboards cutting across the waves. To a non-participant, it looks too wild and rough out there. How can those wet-suited enthusiasts possibly control their direction and speed, and reach their haven safely? It must be possible, however, since some of their

companions are up here on nearby benches, sitting in their wet suits on dry land. Their sailboards are at rest beside them, and they are watching the others on the water with interest, but without concern.

Across the bay are the steel mills of Hamilton, obviously hard at work producing the "million-dollar view" and a lot of more substantial products besides. The Israelites in the wilderness were guided by a pillar of fire by night and a pillar of cloud by day. Our pillars of fire and smoke are also produced around the clock, but just now

The industrial waterfront of Hamilton, seen from the Burlington side of the water

we have no reason to follow them all the way into Hamilton. Instead we proceed a little farther east along the North Shore to visit a piece of Hamilton that, along with Aldershot and part of East Flamborough, came within Burlington's boundaries in the amalgamation of 1958—La Salle Park.

Sixty acres (over 24 ha) of wooded playground on the shores of Burlington Bay were acquired by the Hamilton Parks Department in 1912; this is the grandest estate on the North Shore. The immense old red oaks, identified by Burlington Horticultural Society labels as Honour Roll Trees, are reminders that this park once bordered on

Oaklands, a private estate. Eighty years ago, developers and city fathers alike recognized that this recreational playground would attract commerce and industry, workers and residents to the Hamilton and Burlington area. People from miles around were drawn to this park. They came to ride the roller-coaster, to share immense potluck suppers and church picnics, to go to the cinemas, to swim in the bay. A bathhouse was built down by the shore. There were reports in *The Herald*, nevertheless, of the scandalous news that boys had been seen swimming without appropriate bathing costumes. The ferryboat—the *Macassa* and later the *Lady Hamilton*—regularly linked the park and the Hamilton side of the bay. When the last ferry left at 10:30 P.M., the dancing stopped. Still, some of the most enchanted evenings were danced away in the Pavilion. A year or two later, Toronto came up with Sunnyside Pavilion, but our pavilion has a special charm. From ground level, the wooded bank hides the lake, and the view through the classical colonnades and graceful arcades is green and leafy. From the dance floor upstairs, casement windows used to open out to romantic views of the waters of the bay, reflecting city lights, starlight and moonlight.

Some time in the fifties, people gave up dancing—can this be true?—and structural alterations were made to the Pavilion. The staircase to the upper level was closed off and the windows boarded shut. Eventually the lovely building began to decline into a rather neglected-looking shelter from the rain, a concession, canteen spot, and location for public facilities. Then three years ago it appeared that the La Salle Park Pavilion might be demolished and replaced by an insignificant functional building. It was soon obvious, however, that people wanted the Pavilion to stay. Funds for rebuilding it were raised by many volunteers. There were raffles, dance-a-thons, barbeques, song-and-

dance shows. A competition was organized to paint the hoarding panels around the condemned structure. An amazing variety of murals drew many admirers and amateur art critics to the park and proved once again that creative energies are stronger forces than apathy. Aldershot has always been a vital community, and with this project, the rest of the Burlington could participate in that vitality.

Phase I of the restoration project was completed in June 1994. The hoardings came down and a big ribbon went up, to be cut by le Sieur de la Salle himself, who, reports had it, was intending to return for the occasion by boat. Finally the festive opening day arrived. The more impatient among us thronged down to the dock in anticipation of his long-awaited return. On the way we passed an immense granite stone, placed by the Wentworth Historical Society in 1923, with a bronze plaque commemorating "the landing near this spot in September 1699 of Sieur de la Salle, French explorer, believed to have been the first white man to set foot on these shores." We passed the clubhouse of the Burlington Sailing & Boating Club and signs for the club sailing school. We arrived at the marina, where the boat slips were filled with sailboats, all sails furled. Too rough for sailing. Instead, a steady but syncopated musical rhythm, like wind chimes but with the liveliness of Trinidadian steel drums, the sounds of ropes and cables clanging against aluminum masts, kept us entertained while we waited. There were gulls, mallards, Canada geese with goslings—perhaps the original La Salle saw these, too. We saw our usual great view of rust and smoke, and then, a small, motor-powered craft heading our way. We cheered. La Salle in long wig and brocade coat stepped out onto the dock, opened his arms in an eighteenth-century gesture of greeting, and declared in twentieth-century English, "It's good to be back."

"La Salle lives again" was the front-page story in the Burlington section of *The Spectator*. The seventy-seven-year-old Pavilion was very much alive that evening. Tickets for the Down by the Bay dinner–dance had been sold out for weeks. There were some, they say, who dined and danced with partners from their teens. There were others who have forgotten (or so they say) the names of those earlier dream dates. But all agree that Phase II, the restoration of the dance floor, must not be delayed. More fund-raising and a greater wealth of community memories.

And then—is it too much to hope for the launching and docking of the *Macassa II*, or the *Lady Hamilton II*? After all, the municipal boundary between Hamilton and Burlington is no barrier to conviviality. Many who used to get on the *Lady Hamilton* and come to La Salle Park for a picnic or dancing at the Pavilion now live in Burlington. And other romances have led some people to take up residence in Hamilton, and live there happily ever after. So, in the spirit of good harmony between neighbours, we raise a toast to La Salle and say, *Vive les bons temps!*

If La Salle can set foot on these shores again after three centuries, surely we may anticipate the return of fancy footwork to a waterfront nightspot. It is not so long ago that most non-residents of Burlington knew the town only as a place to go dining and dancing. The Brant Inn in downtown Burlington on the Lakeshore Road most elegantly accommodated a thousand diners and dancers, either on the Lido Deck or, in fine weather, on the floor of

Facing page: Escarpment rocks
gathering moss, near the Mountain Brow Road
Above: New estates in Kilbride

the open-air Sky Club. From the 1920s to the 1950s, under the direction of Murray Anderson and Cliff Kendall, the Brant Inn's reputation for outstanding entertainment spread far and wide. Big-name big bands and great performers played many repeat engagements there: Lena Horne, Ella Fitzgerald, Sophie Tucker, Louis Armstrong, Benny Goodman, Duke Ellington, Count Basie, Tommy and Jimmie Dorsey, the Ink Spots, Xavier Cugat. No doubt they announced, on each return to the Brant Inn bandstand, "It's good to be back." The Sky Club was built out over the lake, and the Lido Deck, designed to resemble a cruise ship, had staterooms for the use of visiting musicians. Fats Waller, a regular performer, is said to have started each day with a pre-breakfast swim—always proclaiming fortissimo as he dashed into the water, "Lake On-ta-a-a-rio, here I come!"

The Brant Inn was closed and demolished just after the New Year's celebration of 1969, but it is a living memory for thousands of dancers, most of whom don't believe the dancing has to stop. It's been a long intermission, but we are ready for the next dance.

Above: Mount Nemo, seen from Walker's Line. Facing page: Harvest home on Walker's Line

CHAPTER FIVE

MOUNT NEMO

Mount Nemo offers the best viewpoints between Toronto and Hamilton. One lookout point, enclosed within a manmade stone-and-concrete wall and provided with benches, is easily accessible along a cleared road allowance from the roadside parking area at the Guelph Line. The Halton Region Conservation Authority does well to invite so many people to share this view. From this promontory on the Niagara Escarpment, you can see a great panorama, limited only by the curvature of the planet and interrupted by a few local irregularities. To the north lies the imposing Rattlesnake Point. To the east, on a clear day, the CN Tower beckons. To the south and west is half of Burlington, then the waters of Lake Ontario, and the Escarpment again on the far side of the lake. The turkey vultures, soaring in spirals on currents of air created by the Escarpment face, may have better views, but I doubt it. They are probably only thinking of where their next meal is coming from. (So look alive.) Anyway, as artists know, the true appreciation of landscape views depends on the contrasting effect created by features silhouetted in the foreground. There is no need to take up hang-gliding, then. Instead, turn off the road allowance to follow a portion of the Bruce Trail up Mount Nemo.

The blazes of the Bruce Trail are easy to follow. The footpath to the left, from the road allowance along the hydro line, leads you into a woods of tall, tall maples and beeches. Through their crowns a few rays of sunshine filter to the mossy, ferny, stony floor of the woods. As you walk up to the Escarpment edge, the rocks are more and more fissured by erosion, until they begin to open into deep crevices. Here some trees cling to the rock, clutching, with their gnarled roots exposed to the open air. The cracks are very deep, and wide enough for a small person

Above: A timber-frame barn. Facing page: At the edge of the Bruce Trail, on Mount Nemo

to fall into. Or even to enter into purposefully, to explore and mine the hidden treasures of the dark underworld. You begin to think of trolls and gnomes. Then you meet some welcome representatives of reality: a couple of spelunkers, carrying a coil of rope, looking down speculatively at passages in the vertical caves. People who know how to do such things actually do enter such crevices, crawl deep inside the escarpment, and intrude upon the various species of bats that live there.

For most people, the mere thought of these hidden depths is enough. And now, almost suddenly, you step out of this chiaroscuro world and find yourself at the edge of a great bowl of light. You look out into this bright space, around and between the trunks of trees that hang on the edge, precariously claiming their share of light that other trees snug in the woods have to reach so high for. You look down through the trees. Far below you see model-sized barns and houses and cars on Walkers Line. There are small fields and fences and hedgerows—"hardly hedgerows, little lines / Of sportive wood run wild." So Wordsworth is here, at least for those who have been made to memorize "Tintern Abbey." "These steep and lofty cliffs, / That on a wild secluded scene impress / Thoughts of more deep seclusion…" How did Wordsworth find so much to say? Mostly words fail us in wild secluded scenes. And when you meet someone on the trail—as you almost certainly will at the lookout point—what will you say as you look out over the miniature golf course, complete with miniature golfers? "Great view, eh?" But the deeper thoughts, however wordless, are here too. As the poet said, you take those thoughts back home with you.

The cleared road allowance that you follow back to the car is a quarry road. Thirty-some years ago, a quarry operation had plans to break through the face of Mount Nemo. They intended to blow it away, but the Halton Region

Conservation Authority acquired the property to preserve it. Preservation in this case means allowing the rock to crumble away at a more natural pace.

Shortly afterwards, a provincial committee was formed to consider the significance and future of this rather well-known and prominent rocky ridge, which is an exposed cuesta of dolomite originally formed on the sea floor of a

Facing page: On the Bruce Trail. Above: Below Mount Nemo

tropical Silurian sea in the Michigan Basin, some 430 to 415 million years ago. After fifteen years of deliberation, the Niagara Escarpment Plan was approved. The threat to Mount Nemo played a role in developing awareness of the need for conservation planning for the Niagara Escarpment. In 1990, when the escarpment was proclaimed a World Biosphere Reserve by UNESCO, the premier of Ontario declared it one of the province's "treasures," a natural feature "that dramatically enhances the quality of life for the people living in this great province. We are determined that the natural and human heritage aspects associated with this unique and valuable feature will be preserved for our children and grandchildren in perpetuity."

It may be difficult for most of us to wrap our minds around the idea of "in perpetuity," or even around the somewhat smaller idea of 430 million years. But on occasion, some human minds are capable of moving fast enough. They recognized and preserved the true wealth of Mount Nemo for the enjoyment of a few more generations.

Looking out from this high point for the CN Tower—there it is!—the thought may occur to you that *that* well-known landmark was built with concrete derived from quarries. Further contemplation, perhaps about seclusion, identity and community, will surely follow.

Above: The Lowville Mill. Facing page: Limestone Hall

CHAPTER SIX

TWELVE MILE CREEK

A river runs through it" is an evocative phrase. Norman Maclean's book of that title, in which he meditates on the pleasures of fly-fishing and the passages of human life, resonates with that old idea of the river of life. No river runs through Burlington. But a topographical map of this territory will show a great many blue lines rising in the uplands, streaming down the Escarpment, carving out ravines, winding and finding their way at last to the lake. Creeks. Many of them have picked up names along the way, some from early settlers, some from neighbouring topographical features: Hager, Rambo, Tuck, Sheldon, Roseland, Shoreacres, Limestone, Falcon, Appleby. And there are many others not named on the map, tributaries with names that only the locals know. Many of these creeks are narrow and shallow; after the spring thaw and runoff, many become mere trickles of water.

Nevertheless, as the name of Grindstone Creek reminds us, some of them have been very hard-working. A hundred and more years ago, Grindstone Creek ran through Smokey Hollow. Smoky indeed, as sawmills, flour mills, a woollen mill, carding mills, tanneries, asheries, foundries, turning shops, and a basket factory crowded around a complex of dams and raceways—and then turned to steam power when water privileges became hard to acquire. Seventeen smokestacks crammed into a half square-mile (just over 1 km²). Nowadays, there is no smoke in Smokey Hollow. All that water power has gone into retirement. Power is carried here from Niagara Falls, and nuclear plants, by way of great lines and colossal towers. But the retirement of Burlington's creeks is like a lot of people's retirements. How does it feel to have nothing to do? Well,

The Twelve Mile Creek at Lowville Park

many retirees find that they keep as busy as ever, but their business is more enjoyable. Just so with the creeks. They no longer power the mills of heavy industry. For the present, their economic benefits are environmental and recreational.

Grindstone Creek is now recognized again, after a period of some neglect, as a great resource. Its restoration forms part of a $7.5-million Fish and Wildlife Habitat Restoration Project for the Hamilton Harbour. The final two miles of the creek flow through the Hendrie Valley, part of the lands of the Royal Botanical Gardens and the locale of many of the RBG's nature trails. In the midst of raising $4 million for Project Paradise, to restore Cootes Paradise—another of its properties, though beyond Burlington's municipal boundaries—the RBG is conscious of the input from Grindstone Creek into that marshy backwater paradise and is working to protect pike-spawning and nursery habitats in the creek. It is a magnificent project, and the creek is worth such a big-money investment.

The best-known creek in Burlington is officially named Bronte Creek, but still generally called Twelve Mile Creek. Just 12 miles (about 20 km) from an opening in the sand strip, right by Joseph Brant's house, that divides the lake from the bay, the creek empties into the lake at Bronte, a neighbouring community that is now part of Oakville. Bronte was named, not after the novel-writing sisters in Yorkshire, but as a tribute to Lord Nelson, whose exploits were also celebrated in the naming of Nelson Township. There is nothing to be said against his honourary Italian title, Bronte, but until the 1930s, when the name was changed by the Ontario Geographic Names Board, the creek was always known as The Twelve. The insignificant fact that there is another Twelve Mile Creek somewhere else does not generally concern those who know which creek they are talking about. It is this creek that is the best example of what may be called active retirement.

Let us follow a route going upstream. Not literally, since that would involve trespassing on private property and encountering numerous hazards, but an imagined journey, following the creek through Burlington's distinctive villages. This has been a hard-working creek, bringing prosperity to several small, concentrated communities. Near the mills, churches were built, and schools, and general stores. Now there are fewer buildings, fewer people in the villages, and almost everyone goes to work somewhere else. The creek has become a place for recreation.

The route begins in Bronte Creek Provincial Park, of which only a corner is within Burlington. The gorge is deep here, and the wooded banks are indeed a gorgeous sight in the autumn, displaying colour that seems every year to be more vivid than it was the last.

At the former hamlet of St. Anns, or Tansley, where Dundas Street crosses the gorge, the steep banks go down 120 feet (37 m) on both sides. The old bridge used to be at the bottom. Or rather, the old series of bridges, as they kept getting washed out. Tansley was the place where travellers stopped to rest up before or after crossing the creek. There was a good-sized hotel, and a guest house to accommodate any extras. After the Department of Highways put in a higher-level bridge, some seventy-five years ago, travellers no longer needed to stop to work up their courage, or to recover. The hotel's gone, of course. But much of the rest of Tansley is still there. It is just that everyone is driving through the place so fast that they do not see it. Blink, and you've missed it. Now that Dundas Street is also Highway 5, the alternate route people take to get there (wherever) faster than they would on the QEW, Tansley is no longer a village that encourages you to take it easy.

Zimmerman is more relaxed. This was a village where at one time almost everyone was called Zimmerman. Henry Zimmerman built his house, a flouring mill, a sawmill, a turning factory, and a store; and his sons took up farming and dentistry and Methodism. The former Zimmerman Methodist Church is now the Trinity Baptist Church. The New Zimmerman School has closed and been converted into a house. Some fine Zimmerman houses have been preserved on the sideroads. One of them is on a byway that used to be the Appleby Line before it was diverted. This house, Nether Lane, is still a show-piece of Zimmerman industry; the shiplap siding, shingles, turned posts, and gingerbread were all produced from local wood in Zimmerman's mill and factory. The mills are ruins, however, and the house now nestles (as realtors say) in the restful seclusion of the idyllic creek valley.

Lowville, a little upstream from the confluence of Limestone Creek and Twelve Mile Creek, is by contrast a busy place. Lowville Park is a favourite recreation spot, the ideal location for large family picnics. There is lots of room for playing softball and Frisbee, by way of working up an appetite for a potluck feast. Young children in arms like being carried over to the fence of the neighbouring farm, to watch the young horses running free, showing off their energy. The older kids get their feet wet in the creek, where there's good crayfish-hunting. Sometimes someone tries to float an inflatable boat in the creek, but the water here is too shallow to provide draft for a raft. It is not deep enough even for easy filling of bazooka water-guns. Older folks can walk over the bridges and under the willows, but mostly they just sit and talk.

If by chance the food on the picnic table is not enough to fuel these activities, the Lowville General Store can supply ice cream and cold drinks and even—when the barbeque is set up outside—sausages and burgers hot off the grill. The historic stone schoolhouse, which was retired from school work years ago, has a second career as a Parks and Recreation building, the headquarters for summer day-camp. Lowville Park is also a centre of the Winter Carnival, when Bur Bear hosts sports and games on the Lowville ice and snow.

Just upstream, the mill race, dam and millpond are reminders that there is real power to be harnessed in the creek. The Cleaver Mill, built in 1837, operated night and day in the nineteenth century, providing plenty of work, and was one of the centres of Lowville's flourishing economic development. Even up to 1957, villagers and visitors could get flour milled there by Norm Langton. Then it was converted into a house—one of the most picturesque homes in all of Burlington.

Upstream from Lowville are the ruins of a house where in 1885 William Delos Flatt courted and married his sweetheart, Rhoda Richardson. Flatt was a highly interesting young man who was to become very wealthy as the principal owner of the largest timber export business in North America. In his memoirs—titled, characteristically, *The Trail of Love*—he tells of bringing his bride home to a log cabin that had only a rag rug on the floor, but they were warmed by happiness. Fifteen years later, after years of hard labour in the forests of Wisconsin, he retired in Burlington. On one of the most beautiful lakeshore estates he built for his wife one of the finest Craftsman-style houses in the whole province: Lakehurst Villa.

In 1924 an unusual tract of land, not far from his wife's childhood home, came up for sale. It was the former site of the Canada Powder Company, bought out in 1862 by the Hamilton Powder Company. The powder-company mill provided great quantities of blasting powder required by the Canadian Pacific Railway when the railway tracks were being carved out of the granite shield of Northern Ontario and the Rocky Mountains of British Columbia.

This mill, like all hard-working mills, worked around the clock, employing in shifts almost every able-bodied man in the villages of Cumminsville, Dakota and Kilbride. There were two hundred employees in 1884. In that year, despite safety precautions—the men never wore hobnailed boots, which would produce devastating sparks—the factory blew up in a tremendous explosion. One lucky worker is said to have lost his false teeth when he was blown into the creek, but they were found again at the Lowville dam. Five men lost their lives, and two hundred their jobs when the company moved its operations to Montreal.

This was the valley—devastated, but then regenerated by the recuperative powers of nature—that was for sale in 1924. Flatt had a vision of "a beautiful summer camp where families can, while within short distances of leading cities, enjoy the peace and contentment found only in the solitudes of nature." The next year he began to build the first of seventy rustic cedar-log cottages. They had stone chimneys, cobblestone fireplaces and—a trademark of the Craftsman style—inglenook seats by the hearth. They also had locally generated electricity, modern sanitation, and rustic cedar garages. The word "developed" does not do full justice to the generous intelligence of Flatt's vision. The layout of the roads and the cottages, the union of private areas with public meeting-spaces, are designed so artfully that the small valley expands into a largesse of space, with every amenity is just a short walk away. And the nine-hole golf course is not at all undersized. All this was accomplished with a minimal use of machinery and a maximal appreciation of the good things of the earth.

Part of the creek was dammed to provide a swimming pond, but those who are not very young and/or warm-blooded usually stay on the beach. When Willbrook Creek, a tributary of The Twelve, was dammed to make a trout pond, Flatt stocked it with thousands of fish. Flatt said, "I

named it Cedar Springs because of the great number of cedars that grow here. The water here is fit for drinking." Clear spring waters gushed from the ground. One spring, the Fountain of Youth, was made immortal in verse by Flatt:

> To a fountain full and deep
> Flowing ever flowing
> Fainting Heart, it is for thee
> Flowing Ever Flowing,
> Ever sparkling, never still
> Taste its sweetness all who will.

The source of the Twelve Mile Creek is still many miles upstream, beyond the boundaries of Burlington. It is tempting to carry on, to visit the ruins of the Dakota Mill—not the powder mill, which left not much more than smithereens—but the gristmill operated by Leonard Pegg until 1978, when it burned to the ground. Now the mill wheel runs nothing at all through a deep romantic chasm, and the cider press is overgrown with meadow flowers. It is tempting too to go up to Kilbride, which has a well-known public well-spring not far from the Kilbride general store. But the Fountain of Youth, with its sense of

Facing page: On Appleby Line
Above: The eye in the cornfield

a secret source of vitality, seems a good stopping-place.

Since 1932 Cedar Springs has been owned by the residents. Flatt, with his vision of "a community camp where the highest ideals of loyalty and citizenship would prevail," retained ownership of just one cottage for the Flatt family.

The Cedar Springs Community Club was set up as an early form of co-operative housing, in which the cottage owners share the costs of maintaining and improving community property. The cottages themselves have changed over the years. Some have aged, some have been renovated, and some have burned down and been replaced. They are still built of wood, mostly cedar, and are rustic in style. Some of them have been occupied by the same family every summer since 1925. And a few summer romances have resulted in marriages and new generations of cottagers. "Flowing ever flowing…"

Facing page: In the greenhouse at the Burlington Art Centre
Above: In the Village Square

The unknown commuter, who just missed his GO train

CHAPTER SEVEN

GOING TO WORK

The people of Burlington are industrious, but there is not much heavy industry here. The smells and other obnoxious aspects of production and manufacturing are few and not well tolerated locally. It is a truth perhaps insufficiently acknowledged, however, that so-called light industry may be more economically productive than more blatantly obvious heavy industry. Even in the nineteenth century, the small workplaces of cities like London and New York produced more than Manchester, Birmingham and other factory cities created by the Industrial Revolution. So Burlington, in a small way, produces a great many goods for world markets: cookies with a definitely Dutch flavour; sophisticated robots; advanced water purification systems; boxes, barrels, baskets, and the most modern kinds of containers; bricks and ceramic tiles and concrete blocks. It is also the headquarters for large national and international corporations selling such goods and services as waste management and transportation. Downtown and all along the QEW are found the head offices of insurance companies, banks and fast-food chains. Add to these the merchants, restaurateurs, garden maintenance crews, copy-shop operators, lawyers, doctors, auto mechanics, and all the others who work right here in the city, and you have a lot of employment.

Nonetheless, this is also a suburb. Since 1912, when William Delos Flatt promoted his vision of Burlington as the "suburb beautiful," it has been a place where most workers have to get out of town to go to work, and then find their way back home at the end of the day, or the job, or the conference. Flatt's promotional booklet for his Lakeshore Surveys includes a photograph of road-grading machines at work on Highway 2, which had been officially opened in 1832 as the Hamilton–York stagecoach route. "The mail-coach between Toronto and Hamilton" was described by Anna Brownell Jameson in her 1838 *Winter Studies and Summer Rambles in Canada* as:

> …a heavy wooden edifice, about the size and form of an old-fashioned lord mayor's coach, placed on runners, and raised about a foot from the ground; the whole was painted of a bright red, and long icicles hung from the roof.
>
> This monstrous machine disgorged from its portal eight men-creatures, all enveloped in bear-skins and shaggy dreadnoughts, and pea-jackets, and fur caps down upon their noses, looking like a procession of bears on their hind legs, tumbling out of a showman's caravan. They proved, however, when undisguised, to be gentlemen, most of them going up to Toronto to attend their duties in the House of Assembly.

Above: Highway 403 and CN freight transport at Aldershot. Facing page: Office windows reflect the dawn on the QEW

One of them, indeed, was introduced to her as Mr. William Johnson Kerr, Joseph Brant's son-in-law and this area's elected member of the Legislative Assembly of Upper Canada since 1820. Winter commuting then was serious business, as Jamieson was at pains to tell her British readers: "Canadian stage-coaches are … heavy, lumbering vehicles, well calculated to live in roads where any decent carriage must needs founder."

In 1912 this historic route was being transformed into a "high-class boulevard road." As Flatt boasted,

> Pine Cove is located on the proposed permanent highway on the Lake Shore Road between Hamilton and Toronto. An hourly service on the Radial Electric Railway from Hamilton, running as far as Oakville is now completed, and cheap rates prevail. It is generally understood that this line of Electric Railway will be continued from Oakville to Toronto. It has also been proposed by people interested in the auto business, that motor busses will be run on the proposed concrete highway, between Hamilton and Toronto. Pine Cove has an unsurpassed location, and offers you the opportunity to own a home in the country, and yet be in close touch with the City. The man of tomorrow is going to live out in the air in the suburbs.

Eighty years later, the people of tomorrow still find Lakeshore Road, now designated an Ontario Heritage Highway, a delightful high-class boulevard, but not the route of choice for going to work. Even the late—it was almost always late—lamented milk-run Lakeshore GO bus does not run, or stop-and-go, here any more. There are still buses to Hamilton and special express buses to McMaster University. But for people with cars, the route is now either the 403, whose long-proposed extension is under construction, or the Queen Elizabeth Way.

The QEW has the heaviest traffic of any roadway in North America. Drivers who get caught in the rush hour, that is, most of the daylight and pre-dawn hours, keep the car radio tuned to a station that reports traffic tie-ups. The luckier commuters have an alternative—the GO train, today's answer to the long-gone Radial line. Ticket in hand, or monthly pass in pocket, GO Transit passengers have their own routines. They leave their cars in the parking lot, or get dropped off at the Kiss and Ride, or catch a free ride to the station with Burlington Transit. They have their preferred coaches, their preferred seats, their preferred newspapers, and their preferred travelling companions. They doze, or open their briefcases and do mental warm-up exercises. They talk. Aspiring playwrights could do worse than eavesdrop on the GO train by way of picking up dramatic dialogue. The rest of the passengers become an unwitting audience. If you lose interest in stories about someone else's fellow workers, or boasts about big deals in the boxes at the Jays games, or complaints from tired guys who "just want a package" and retirement, you can always

Solid brick structures at Canada Brick

slip on headphones and retreat into a private world of pre-recorded sounds.

Or you may be lucky enough to work at home. The home office, equipped with modem, fax, and telephone-answering system, has enabled many workers to forego the monthly GO pass and be just an occasional commuter. Home can be an unsurpassed location for work. You can still keep in touch with the city, or indeed the world, and occasionally combine work-for-income with unpaid homework such as household chores and child care.

Yet another form of home business, one that provides plenty of work for the whole family, can be found in Burlington. This traditional form of industry, for more than a century producing the area's largest export business and its greatest prosperity, is the working farm. A home in the country, despite appearances to the contrary, is not always a suburban idyll. Many old and new farmhouses include the offices or headquarters for industrious and active agricultural production.

When the Society for Industrial Archeology recently produced an excellent book called *Toronto, and Beyond: The SIA Scrapbook, 1994*, Niagara and Hamilton were included as "other destinations," but Burlington got not one mention.

The SIA members are interested in places with steam engines and smokestacks—even (or perhaps especially) if they are no longer working. Barns are apparently not their thing, no matter whether they house modern milking-systems or rusting antique tractors. Nevertheless, the most noteworthy historic palaces of industry and commerce in Burlington are its magnificent timber-frame barns. The barn on the Gunby Homestead on Britannia Road, for instance, was said to be the largest in Ontario. The builder of this and many other local barns was Hal Gunby, who celebrated the completion of every one of them by standing on his head on the roof ridge. Even at the age of eighty-five, after helping reshingle his own barn roof, he insisted on his usual upside-down celebration. Both Gunby and his barns were dedicated to an extended working life.

Burlington barns were built from the resources of the farm; the timbers and the stones for the foundation were gathered there. And they are the size they are because the land was made so productive by farm labour. The sources of power were sun and water, the soil, and a lot of human energy. Old photographs showing the participants in a barn-raising bee—dozens of people perched on a timber frame—reveal just how much employment used to be offered by farming. And much wealth was produced too, because Burlington has soil that is ideal for agricultural industry. People who know how to farm have come here from all over the globe—from Britain, the American colonies and states, the Netherlands, and the Ukraine—and produced goods that have been shipped out all over the globe. Many of them are still at it. Some barns still in use by the third and fourth generations of the same family are identified by roadside signs: Ontario Century Farm.

Question: How does a family stay in farming for a century or more? Answer: By working without stopping.

Farming is a stay-at-home business, but not entirely so.

It is a misperception that the farmer who stays on the farm never goes farther than the back field. The farmer, the farmer's wife, and the whole family go out to work too—at four in the morning, if need be—when produce is delivered to market. At least at that hour they avoid the heavy traffic. And successful farmers, like other responsible captains of industry, go to work for the community too. A century or so ago, there were farmers who gave portions of their land for the building of the first churches and schools, and then they went to board meetings to keep those institutions going. They served on local councils and auxiliaries, and supported good causes.

There are still good causes to serve. In 1992, friends and admirers threw a party for someone described in *The Spectator* as a "retired Burlington farmer." Since his home was still on the farm and the farm was still working, it may be suspected that Brock Harris occasionally continued to do some farm work. Harris was retiring from the Halton Region Conservation Authority, which he had helped to form thirty-one years earlier, and had served as chairman since 1973. When he was hailed as "the moving force behind Halton's conservation movement," Harris commented that the attention made him a little uncomfortable: "I'd sooner be out working in the back field." During those three decades, the HRCA acquired about 8,000 acres (3,240 ha) of conservation areas, and these are visited by more than 400,000 people every year. Many of those visitors will stop at the lookout point at Mount Nemo, which has been named to honour this untiring worker for the cause. Reflecting upon the past achievements of the HRCA, Brock Harris said, "I'm satisfied about what we've done in the past, but there's still a lot left to do…. This is a growing area and it has to have a place for conservation." Spoken just like a farmer, always aware of how much work remains to be done.

Above: The interior of St. Luke's Anglican Church

In the Holy Protection
of the Blessed Virgin Mary
Ukrainian Catholic Church

THE GARDEN OF CANADA

A recent local best-seller is a book published by the Burlington Historical Society that tells the story of the past century of this village/town/city. *Burlington: The Growing Years* tells two stories. The second story is about growth and development in size and population during the past fifty years. The first, or ground-level, story is about the fruit growers, vegetable growers, wheat growers, and nursery workers who nurtured the first hundred years of our prosperity. The land of the Plains and other areas of Burlington south of Dundas Street is not only scenic, but also generous. The sandy loam deposited on the bed of the post-glacial-age Lake Iroquois made wonderfully fertile soil, and present-day Lake Ontario moderates temperatures to produce a Carolinian-zone climate. The result is an ideal place for growing things.

A turn-of-the-century visitor was so inspired by the fertility of this area that she named Burlington and vicinity "The Garden of Canada" in her book of that title, published in 1902. As Martha Craig "inhaled the delightful perfume of the breezes laden with drifts of apple blossoms," she waxed rhapsodic: "Such were my thoughts as I stood, for the first time, on the shores of Burlington Bay, as it lay like a sparkling gem, surrounded by verdant green, reflecting a sky as blue as Italy's. On either side, from the placid shore to the foothills of the protecting mountains, stretched fertile lands on which hundreds of thousands of fruit trees flourish. In this earthly paradise live a happy, rich and prosperous people."

Facing page: Burlington apples for sale at a roadside stand
Right: The family dining-room in the Ireland House Museum

The Fairview farmers' market

There is nothing in Craig's book to contradict her assertion, however euphoric it may sound. Some seventy pages later, the voice of W.A. Emory, Esq., a farmer on the Plains, is more down-to-earth, but just as happy: "The tomato industry has developed most rapidly and wonderfully. Several years ago the writer [that is, Emory himself] grew a few tomatoes and one day took a dozen bushels to Hamilton market and could not dispose of them; had to bring them home and feed them to the hogs. Now the tomatoes are grown by the thousand bushels and consumed in Hamilton by canning factories."

The Garden of Canada illustrates time and again how the farmers of Burlington a century ago secured their prosperity, not only by supporting horticultural advancement and developing new varieties, but also by developing successful ways of marketing and disposing of their crops. Soon farmers were diversifying into basket-making factories, and shipping their fruits to markets in Britain, Europe and South Africa. There was an apple-evaporating factory downtown on Caroline Street, next to the Springer–Bell orchards. In 1903 the Burlington Canning Company built a tomato cannery on the lakeshore, at the foot of Brant Street. For almost sixty years the aroma of ketchup was redolent throughout the downtown during the canning season. A few urban residents did not find its perfume quite as delightful as that of apple blossom. And up until the 1960s, students at McMaster University in Hamilton discovered during freshman initiation week how countless bushels of overripe tomatoes from Burlington were disposed of—as ammunition in the traditional rite of passage known as the Tomato Fight. Sometimes one can have too much of a good thing, even in this earthly paradise.

The copiousness and quality of the fruits that were grown in Burlington orchards were celebrated: apples, cherries, peaches, plums, pears and apricots all grew abundantly. Burlington cantaloupe melons were famous. Along the Plains Road and Maple Avenue, and east along the Lakeshore Road, New Street, and the Middle Road (now the QEW), and in all the cultivated fields in-between, market gardeners grew strawberries, spinach, lettuce, cabbages, beets, carrots, cauliflowers, and, of course, tomatoes. Today the stalls at the Fairview farmers' market and the downtown Burlington market still overflow with an abundance of good things to eat. The gardens that enchanted Craig in 1902 were all located south of Dundas Street, in the area now zoned for urban development. In present-day Burlington, almost all the farms protected by rural land-use zoning are north of Dundas Street.

Murray Fisher struck the right note in his memoir, which he titled "Farewell to the Garden of Canada." As a seven-year-old boy, he saw Martha Craig travelling around Burlington with her horse and buggy and camera, making notes and taking photographs to illustrate her book. Eighty-two years later, retired from a lifetime of farming, he saw the Burlington Mall, parking lot, and market stalls occupying what used to be the Fisher farm and its homestead, Shady Cottage. The neighbouring farms became residential developments; their farmhouses, Locust Lodge and Balsam Lodge, are surrounded by post-war housing; and Ireland House at Oakridge Farm is now a flourishing museum. Murray Fisher's memoir was a fond farewell. He appreciated the great value of the fertile land that had been developed and paved over. He remembered and recorded the names of the families who had worked on 400 farms south of the No. 1 Side Road through many growing years. Of those 400 farms, 375 were long gone by 1984. But the families have continued to grow and add to the growth of Burlington. Those mentioned in The Garden of Canada and "Farewell to the Garden of Canada"—Davis, Fisher, Bell, Lemon, Emery, Peart, Gallagher, Wood, Lindley, Thorpe, Unsworth, Kemp, Smith, Walker, Easterbrook and so many more—have given an inheritance to Burlington's present and future residents.

As Murray Fisher at the end of his ninth decade observed, "To many oldsters who were born or farmed here, there will never be a Garden again like the one of the early 1900s…. Let us have no regrets, up and at 'em young Canada. Accept the new but do not forget the old."

The farms of Maple Avenue have been redeveloped as the Mapleview Centre and residential subdivisions. Even here, shoppers a few decades from now may view mature

Above: Strawberry picking. Facing page: Ready for Christmas in an Unsworth and Son greenhouse

maples, and in the subdivisions gardens will certainly bloom again. People who buy houses built on this wonderful soil often discover a new fascination with gardening. Amateur gardeners accomplish wonders even with small new garden plots, as the Burlington Horticultural Association garden tours and the Civic Rose Awards have recognized. Much expertise and inspiration is provided by the Royal Botanical Gardens, and fine garden-stock is sold by RBG volunteers in their annual May sale and at their garden shop. The enthusiasm, lore, and surplus plants shared by neighbours over the garden fence is even more inspiriting. And there is a growing trend toward planting fruits and vegetables, not just flowers, in our backyards. One downtown garden has become quite famous as a miniature Garden of Eden. It has been cultivated in the past few years right next to a highrise apartment building, on land that used to be a Bell family market-garden. The surplus good things to eat are set out in baskets at the end of the driveway. There are sometimes tomatoes. And yes, they are delicious.

Above: The famous Iris Garden in bloom at the Royal Botanical Gardens
Facing page: The Hendrie Gates at the Royal Botanical Gardens

CHAPTER NINE

THE ROYAL BOTANICAL GARDENS

The RBG has been called "a microcosm of Canadian heritage,"—a label that extends beyond one level of meaning. The Gardens received royal assent in 1930, and in 1941 were named by an Act of Parliament as a provincial institution. Originally within the boundaries of the City of Hamilton, the Gardens now link the regions of Wentworth and Halton. When the plains and valleys of Aldershot joined with Burlington in 1958, the Lilac Dell, the Rock Gardens, the Rock Chapel, and Cootes Paradise all remained on the other side of the border. The remaining 300 or so acres (about 120 ha) of the world's largest botanical garden are within Burlington. We have the Rose Garden; the Laking Garden, full of irises and herbaceous perennials; the RBG Centre and Mediterranean Greenhouse; and the Hendrie Valley. But our experience of the gardens is not limited by dotted lines on municipal maps.

A botanical garden is by definition designed for the scientific study of plants. Transplants from all regions of the world are represented in the collection, and new varieties, cultivars and hybrids are bred and propagated. The RBG's lilies, which offer visitors an extraordinarily fragrant and showy experience, have come from Korea, China, Taiwan and Japan, the Caucasus and the Pyrenees. The irises may be Siberian or African. The many species of clematis, which the guidebook advises are "widely distributed, mostly in East Asia, the Himalayas, and North America," are collected together on trellises and can be viewed in the course of a short stroll through the Hendrie Gardens. In the Rose Garden, a sensuous abundance of ever-more-endearing blooms, the labels inform us that the genetic history of the rose is linked to the power politics of human history—the Roman occupation of Britain, the Crusades, the Tudors, the Bonapartes and the Bourbons—and that

*Inside the Mediterranean Greenhouse at the
Royal Botanical Gardens*

the ancestors of these roses travelled a long way from China and the Middle East and France so that these modern hybrids could put down roots here.

The thousands of people who come to the RBG, including those avid frequent visitors who have purchased memberships, are as international in origin as the plants that live here. Sikhs in turbans may look at Japanese Turk's-Cap lilies. Francophones and anglophones may discuss Ginkgo trees. Languages from around the world are heard amid the irises or in the tea room. You don't have to be English to love roses, or Dutch to appreciate tulips, or Chinese to admire the Chinese Matrimonial Vine. In fact, the RBG is a microcosm of multicultural heritage.

The Mediterranean Greenhouse at the RBG Centre offers another small world: a microclimate where you can take off your jacket in February and enjoy a mini-paradise of jasmine, coffee, lemons, and figs. The local grocery store, it is true, might provide some of these ingredients as well, but not the relaxed, easygoing atmosphere. Nor the bougainvillea, passion flowers, kangaroo paws, and giant ferns. There is nothing like walking into the greenhouse in midwinter and being met by an envelope of warm air saturated with the scent of hyacinths—especially if you have just spent an hour or so walking along the trails of the snow-blanketed Hendrie Valley.

The gardens are not for summer only, but have much to offer year-round. The nature trails are a perennial resource in all seasons, even in February and March when thousands of plants are hidden under ground and snow, their pointed shoots full of determined potential. The Brackenbrae Trail is a favourite. If we had time and leisure to spare, many of us would walk it almost daily throughout the calendar year and never tire of it. When there is nothing in bloom, there is still much to look for. You'll see cardinals, grosbeaks and jays; chickadees that take seeds from your open hand; and the huge pileated woodpecker with its huge appetite hungrily scrounging deep in a hollow tree. The winter light, the leafless trees, the frozen waters of Grindstone Creek and the swamp—all provide a landscape as absorbing and full of interest as the charm of springtime wildflowers.

The Hendrie Valley is a wildlife sanctuary, meant to provide habitats for a rich diversity of both animal and plant life. The sanctuary areas are in this respect unlike the Mediterranean Greenhouse, where the only animals to be observed are the goldfish in the little pool. The large-scale map of the world, located just outside the greenhouse and showing the RBG as the smallest of the Mediterranean climate zones, displays a delightful fiction. The greenhouse is not a whole ecosystem, but only a botanical preserve. In some ways, it is similar to a zoological garden. At the zoo, animals live in an incomplete environment and have to wait for feeding time. The RBG natural lands, however, are home to a large population of some one thousand wild plant species, whose numbers are limited only by their ability to get their own living. They get their own food and provide for other hungry appetites.

These wild plants include many native to this area—the trillium, the skunk cabbage, the jack-in-the-pulpit, even the giant ragweed of Lamb's Hollow. Look up and see the native trees of Canada—the oaks, the hickories, the hemlock, and the sugar maple, emblem dear of its home and native land. Look down and see the bloodroot, *Sanguinaria canadensis*, the most Canadian of wildflowers. Whereas the botanical part of the gardens is absolutely dependent on imported stock, the wild plant species in the sanctuaries have come by chance and hardiness; they are co-dependent and competitive. Some of these are not welcome, indeed some are labelled "invasive aliens." Purple loosestrife, the best-known alien, has a popular reputation little better than that of dangerous creatures from outer space. Having "gained a foothold" in our marshes, will it go on to invade and take over our gardens, our country, our planet Earth?

Those not wishing to pursue that particular scenario any further have another paradox to consider. As the RBG Nature Interpretation Co-ordinator reports, "native species are known to run amok as well." The touch-me-not, with its explosive seed-pods, has been touched experimentally by so many thousands of delighted schoolchildren, that it is "spreading rapidly and usurping the habitat of other native wildflowers." People who come here to observe and learn cannot help but alter the natural environment that offers them so much enjoyment. More than 100,000 visitors each year have a powerful impact on the life of the plants and animals—natives and newcomers—that now make their home in the RBG lands.

Facing page: Snowed in on Locust Street
Above: A Burlington garage sale

Above: Waiting for a turn at bat. Facing page: Soccer in Central Park

CHAPTER TEN

PARKS AND RECREATION

No doubt every department at City Hall works in its own way for our health, security and welfare, but the efforts of the Parks and Recreation Department staff are the most popularly appreciated, for their business is to provide for our full enjoyment of our leisure time. City parks, large and small, are sites for a great variety of recreational activities.

Bayview Park, for instance, up the Escarpment off King Road, offers not only a fine view of the bay but also wide-open skies. A mini-airport and runway, scaled for model airplanes, accommodates members of the Burlington Radio Controlled Modelers club. Beginners in a training program, earning their wings, and longtime fliers—juniors and retirees—all share an enthusiasm for vicarious aerial manoeuvres. According to a story in the *Burlington Post*, the *Able Mabel*, a 13-foot (4-m) replica modelled on a Lancaster that flew 132 successful missions in the Second World War, had by 1994 reached a total of 134 flights without a crash. "Please don't use the C word," plead the club members.

In other parts of Burlington, boys on BMX bikes speed around dirt tracks. Young people practise the martial arts of aikido, karate, and tae kwon do. Lawn bowlers make an idyllic picture of green and white in their Central Park set-ting near the Seniors' Recreation Centre. Long summer evenings fill the softball diamond in nearby Lions' Park with enthusiastic players and the bleachers with cheerers-on of girls' leagues—the atoms, squirts, and novices. Burlingtonians are into fitness. This is where Participaction is at, although we like spectator sports, too—the extra-long GO trains are always filled to capacity for Blue Jays home games at the Skydome.

*Top: Winter
Carnival in
Lowville Park*

*Below: The Robbie
Burns Day Run*

The wide variety of recreational programs administered by the City complement the many amenities offered by private fitness clubs, and innumerable free-lance activities. There's hockey year-round at the Mainway Arena, skating outdoors in winter at Lowville Park, gymnastics centres in Maple Park, climbing and swinging on the structures at the tiny nameless playground near St. Luke's Church. There's soccer at Sherwood Forest Park, the Burlington Hornets Basketball Clubs, and volleyball on the sand at Beachway Park. Wading and splashing outdoors in Nelson and La Salle Parks. Serious aqua-fit and competitive swimming in the indoor pools at the Y, Angela Coughlan, Aldershot, or Burlington Centennial. Tennis. Golfing. Cyclists in serious bicycling gear on serious bikes keep on going up and down country roads, undeterred by the Escarpment. Moms and dads and the kids, with big and little bikes and safety helmets, pedal along the bikeways and take in the scenery. Sailing and other kinds of boating offer the pleasure of being out on the water and new perspectives of the lakeshore. There's such a wealth of choices—different degrees of physical workout, different sorts of focus and achievement—but all contributing to a restoring and strengthening of body and spirit.

The Around-the-Bay Race, through Hamilton and Burlington, is the earliest and longest-running footrace in North America. We enjoy a kind of vicarious accomplishment in the achievements of our more famous runners. In a single summer, one Burlington woman ran at the Commonwealth Games in Victoria, and another came to British Columbia at the triumphant conclusion of a cross-country run from a starting point in Newfoundland, wearing out many pairs of shoes. Exemplary runners, these women came back to a city where groups of more run-of-the-mill runners continue to puff along quiet streets and paths.

Parks designed for so-called passive use—the less aerobically challenging exercises of walking the dog, strolling hand-in-hand, or just sitting on a park bench—also boost our energies and spirits. Along the shoreline, a newly regenerated Waterfront Trail links eight City-owned parks and "windows to the lake." The smaller "windows" include the Bayshore Park on North Shore Boulevard, with its view of the Skyway, the Canada Centre for Inland Waters, and industrial Hamilton. Along the Lakeshore Road are Burloak Park, with its occasional views of the Skylon Tower at Niagara Falls and lakers docking at the pier of the Petro-Canada refinery in Oakville; Sioux Lookout Park, where ducks and Canada geese meet at the mouth of Roseland Creek; and Port Nelson Park, once the site of a busy agricultural shipping industry and now the most romantic of picnic spots.

Spencer Smith Park links the downtown with the Beach Strip, making a stretch of public waterfront almost 2 miles (over 3 km) long. Spencer Smith Park is Burlington's boardwalk—a place for people and dogs to greet acquaintances. Watching the water and the weather is endlessly fascinating. You can study the rough or smooth reflections of the light of the sky, the moon, and the lights of the Skyway. There are also things to look for in and on the water—fish, cormorants, gulls, sailboats, motorboats and great tankers. On land, amateur jugglers, buskers, and even an occasional storyteller attract audiences. In summertime the onshore breezes moderate the heat of the day, the benches are comfortable, and the ice-cream cones are appealing. In wintertime those breezes, in their fiercer moods, create fantastic ice sculptures on the lamp standards, and walkers move as briskly as they can to avoid becoming ice sculptures themselves.

In three city parks, historic buildings have been conserved for reuse. The stone schoolhouse in Lowville Park,

the Pump House at Beachway Park—a celebration of twentieth-century engineering in Romanesque and Beaux-Arts style—and the La Salle Pavilion, all heritage structures, add distinctive character to their surroundings. Burlington's most recent parkland acquisition, the Shoreacres Estate, offers even greater possibilities—and a great challenge. What will be made of it? Almost everyone who has visited the 14-acre (5.6 ha) estate agrees that it is a delightful combination of natural preserve and artfully designed landscape. The mouth of Shoreacres Creek and preserved wetlands, which have attracted migrant birds annually for centuries now, are the only

such unspoiled resource in this part of Ontario. The rest of the landscape and the mansion and outbuildings provide a series of delightful surprises and "secret garden rooms," set apart from the great lake-view. The open paddock, the shaded paddock, the stables, tennis courts, and children's playhouse are evocative of an era of privileged leisure activity.

In 1930, when Edythe Birge McKay used her inheritance from her father, who was a founding director of Stelco, to build a luxurious residence on her summer property, her architects and landscape designers transformed but did not obliterate its earlier character. Originally part of

a crown grant in 1809 to Laura Secord (*the* Laura Secord), the Shoreacres Estate was the creation of W.D. Flatt: "This is where enjoyment to the fullest may be had; the environment as it were, being amongst the pines, beautiful fruit trees with a sandy beach, and the pure waters of Lake Ontario, all at your command."

The house and garden design is a creative integration of tradition and modernism. The old gatehouse was retained, and the McKay mansion incorporated the old farmhouse into its grand new structure. The former McKay–McNichol family summer estate is to be transformed once again—but this time without the financial

Facing page: Sailboats on the lake
Above: Lawn bowling in Central Park

cushion of a great family fortune. Closed up and dormant, as if for a long winter, the estate has a Sleeping Beauty atmosphere. The time may come when "enjoyment to the fullest may be had" and shared again by Burlingtonians and other visitors to this magnificent estate, which has the potential to become one of the great municipal parks of Ontario.

Above: In the Burlington Art Centre sculpture studio

CHAPTER ELEVEN

ARTS AND LETTERS

The Burlington Art Centre has well-appointed and spacious galleries where temporary exhibitions are installed for free public viewing. The BAC also has space to display a fine collection of contemporary ceramic art—in styles ranging from magnificent vases and elegant teapots to grossly realistic representations like *Spring Pantry*, with its shelves full of preserves that have been overlooked for far too long. Other funky favourites are *King Cow,* and *Vincent Draws a Crowd*—a ceramic revision of a Van Gogh self-portrait, in the form of a three-dimensional bust with a single ear. These high-art ceramics take as their starting point either the fine porcelain container that is much too precious to use, or the kitschy, useless souvenir object, and elevate it to the status of objet d'art—technically sublime and/or wittily ridiculous. But the Art Centre is a gallery with a difference. When you enter the building, you cannot help noticing that it hums with the energy of volunteers. Of course, many art galleries in other cities also depend on committee volunteers to operate their gift shops and picture-rental

services, and to act as docents. The difference here is that, aside from the ceramics acquisitions and the exhibition program, this is a centre built by the volunteer efforts of practising artists and craftspeople. The patrons and collectors take second place to the creators.

Some two hundred years ago William Blake, in his creative memoir about how he learned the craft of printmaking and became an artist, observed that two separate "portions of human existence"—"the Prolific" and "the Devourer" (whom we more politely call the consumer)—are essential

The Burlington Teen Tour Band on parade down Brant Street

to each other. Of course, collectors and patrons are necessary for the survival of the arts and of all artists who depend upon their artistry to make their living. What is intriguing in the BAC is the demonstration of the plain fact that creativity, "the active springing from Energy," as Blake called it, can thrive as a volunteer and not-for-profit activity. It is fascinating to see what can be accomplished by so-called amateurs and craftspeople who gain their livelihood in other ways, once commercial motivation is set aside.

The Art Centre was built because of the efforts of the guilds. In the 1970s, Arts Burlington, a group combining the volunteer energies of many people active in various crafts guilds, raised funds and gathered support for the building of a centre with superb studio facilities. These studios are the home of the guilds: the Burlington Potters Guild, the Latow Photographers Guild, the Burlington Handweavers & Spinners Guild, the Burlington Guild of Sculptors and Wood Carvers, the Burlington Fine Arts Association, and the Burlington Hooking Craft Guild. The weavers' looms set up in one studio, the decoy sculptors' tables and tools in another, the pots in progress, the darkroom—all form part of communal work-spaces, where creativity is exercised and expressed not in isolation but in a group where the lore and learning of their art are shared. And the studios interconnect in productive ways. The Textile Studio has windows looking into the tropical greenhouse, where bougainvillea, hibiscus, oleander, and an almost apocalyptic *Datura*—angels' trumpets—are tended by volunteers.

Annual Kaleidoscopes open these workshops so that the public can view the various artists at work. Some of the artworks on display are for sale, but a major appeal for many visitors is the recognition that they too could practise these arts. The courses offered "for the absolute beginner" are for adults as well as children. The studios are also used by visiting school-classes, some six thousand students every year. On one school-day visit, the Pottery Studio is filled with students rather noisily aroused by the sensation of manipulating mud—something they may not have done since they were little kids. In the Fine Arts Studio across the way, an intent silence prevails, as those who are trying out basket-weaving concentrate on the ins and outs of their frames and fibres. The goal of the BAC—"to encourage community involvement in the arts from all walks of life"— is well summed up in the name of its gift shop, the Art Connection. People do connect with art here, as active participants. Through both their failures and their successes they find sources of vitality and energy that can be tapped only through personal engagement with the arts.

The experience of the visual arts in Burlington is paralleled in the theatre arts and in music. The Teen Tour Band, which plays at almost every celebratory and festive occasion in Burlington, and travels the world as well, comprises amateur young players supported by enthusiastic volunteer fund-raising. The band continues to grow in scope and achievement, and this young tradition is the more impressive because the band members, after all, are teens for only a few years. The Burlington Little Theatre provides entertainment for audiences and a lot of creative energy for the amateur players, on- and off-stage. For the most part, the arts in Burlington are participatory. Some professional artists have had their beginnings here (but Robert Bateman has gone west), and others have moved here. But for the great names in music, theatre, dance and art, we generally get on the GO train or the QEW and go to Toronto for a night out.

Literature is different. To take in the works of great men and women of letters we don't have to get out of town— all we need are their printed words. Curled up with a book by Gabriel Garcia Marquez or Alice Munro, we can travel

Ceramic figures and reflections in the Burlington Art Centre

through time and space. The Burlington Public Library has provided books for borrowers since 1872. According to a note in *The Garden of Canada* by Library Committee Trustee O.T. Springer, in that year, "The sum of $56 was spent in books, etc.… The trustees appropriated a further sum of $25 in 1873. These were the initial movements towards funding a library, and seem to have satisfied the people for some time, as no further grants were made until January, 1883, when $33 was granted and expended."

The BPL has come a long way since those early times. As the city continues to grow, the Library branches out.

The next branch library we build will have a swimming pool and gymnasium right next-door—providing for both mental and physical exercise.

Oddly enough, another well-known literary venue is the Burlington Golf and Country Club. For almost a quarter century, prominent authors have been coming to Burlington to read from their publications at the "Book and Author" series sponsored by A Different Drummer Books. It is, in fact, the longest-running author reading series in the country. A variety of visiting personalities, from Pierre Berton to the Cat in the Hat, have also visited our local

bookshop. The wealth of books on the shelves attracts not only the people of Burlington and environs, but even long-distance customers in Monaco and the Northwest Territories. Over the years, these constant and curious readers have acquired their own personal libraries and, along the way, a collection of bookmarks with the familiar quotation from Henry David Thoreau: "If a man does not keep pace with his companions, perhaps it is because he hears a different drummer. Let him step to the music which he hears, however measured or far away."

Some books, such as dictionaries, are necessities. Some are workouts for the mind—as Thoreau described them, "what we have to stand on tiptoe to read and devote our most alert and wakeful hours to." And some are complete pleasure. Like music, dance and the visual arts, they fill our lives with the shared riches of other people's experience.

Above: The Burlington Summer Festival celebrated in top hat and tails—and informal dress

CHAPTER TWELVE

FESTIVAL DAYS

Most of Burlington's festivals are celebrated downtown, in the heart of the city. The BAC Arts and Crafts Fair is held on a summer weekend in Spencer Smith Park. Just a short walk from this park—up the green, tree-lined vista known as Church Avenue—is the white frame St. Luke's Anglican Church, built in 1832. The St. Luke's Festival, held each May or June, features music, folk dancing on the green, guided tours of the decorated church interior, more music, a tour of the historic graveyard—where the guide may, if so inclined, reveal some long-buried historical secrets—and more music. From the churchyard, the volunteers of the Local Architectural Conservation Advisory Committee lead walking tours of heritage streetscapes, and houses built by Jabez Bent, George Blair, and A.B. Coleman. The favourite is always Coleman's own Gingerbread House, a celebration of every decorative element available to builders a century ago. Then we head back into the church for more music.

The annual Sound of Music Festival features a grand parade of many visiting bands marching down Brant Street, led by our own Burlington Teen Tour Band. The downtown streets stay closed to traffic for the weekend. Outdoor concerts and rockfests fill the streets with crowds by day and by night. On Canada Day Burlington is edged with an animated red-and-white border as the waterfront parks come alive with celebrants. The red-jacketed Teen Tour Band can hardly compete with the great medley of red-and-white T-shirts, sun-hats and ensembles worn by thousands of Canadian patriots, all carrying miniature flags.

For good eating, the Multicultural Festival is not to be missed. Do *not* eat lunch before you go. The spirited Ukrainian dancers, the limbo artists from the Caribbean, and the Highland Scottish sword-dancers are wonderful to see on the outdoor stage, with the lake beyond. The true ethnic experience, however, is best celebrated in consuming the many delightful varieties of home-cooking. For a multicultural feast, try homemade perogies, sausages, curries, ginger beer, and baklava. Later on in the year, the Ukrainian Catholic church hall will open its doors so that we may stuff ourselves with cabbage rolls; L'Eglise St. Philippe will do likewise in December so that we may enjoy homemade tourtière and pea soup. Of course it is always possible to eat very well in Burlington, but these occasional feasts are particularly exotic and memorable.

In 1994 the Sound of Music Festival was enhanced by a special cultural event—the celebration of the fifth anniversary of the twinning of the city of Burlington with

Itabashi, Japan. Thanks to the volunteers of the Mundialization Committee and our visitors from Itabashi, we could see traditional Japanese folk-dancing, martial arts, and drumming, and drink authentic fine Japanese tea. On the evening of June 18th the waterfront parks filled with thousands of people, so many people that it seemed every resident of Burlington had turned out, each bringing a guest. The attraction was the Itabashi Friendship Fireworks display, a gift from our twin city, long famed for its artistry in pyrotechnics. The evening was hot, even by the lakeside, but we packed ourselves in and sat down in quiet expectation as the sunlight faded from the sky and the lake. Reflected in the darkening water were the lights of the Skyway, and the signal lights of many little boats poised out-of-range of the barge holding the explosives and technicians. And then, after a few speeches and expressions of mutual friendship and good will between the twin cities, the show began.

Everyone knows about the excitement and beauty of fireworks, but this show had an added dimension. It was as if the paintings on a Japanese screen or scroll from the seventeenth century were being put into motion. The dark sky was the traditional gold-leaf background, and the liquid flow of fiery and fading light was the ink of traditional calligraphy.

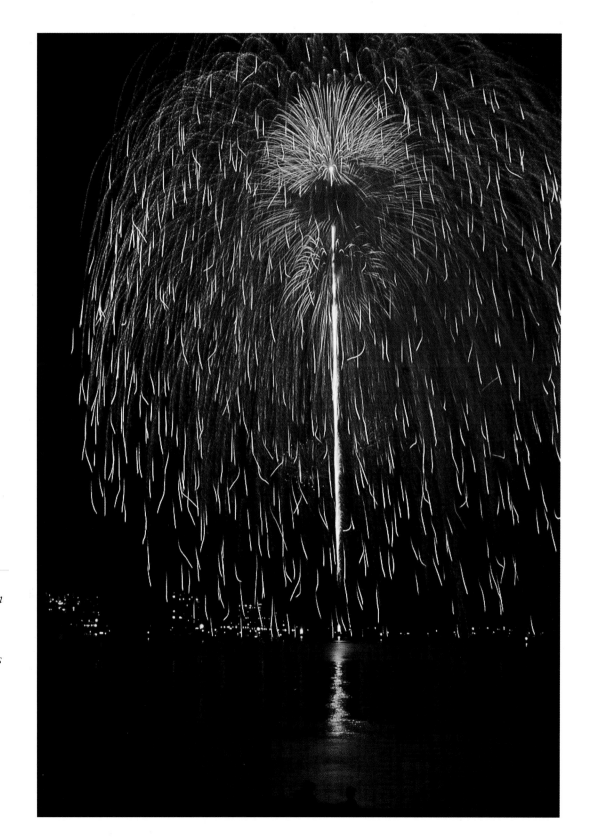

Facing page: The Burlington Teen Tour Band in the Santa Claus Parade

Right: Friendship Fireworks presented by the city of Itabashi, Japan

The controlled spontaneity of these cursive lines was superb. We were awed. Japan is a nation that takes particular care to protect and preserve artifacts recognized as "important art objects" or "important cultural property." The artistry and technical skills celebrated in these national treasures were also, we were privileged to see, brought into play for our fireworks show—an event that lasted less than an hour, and then vanished into dust. But time seemed suspended while we were watching. And afterwards, the spectacle was put away in our memories, recalled not so much in sight and sound, as in the pleasure we experienced. For such a timeless gift, we can only say thank you—*domo arigato gozaimasu*—to our friends in Itabashi.

Not a twin city exactly, but a friendly competitor we meet annually in the Burlington International Games, is our namesake in Vermont. Why we share our civic name has not been determined—perhaps for no other reason than that it is a good name. "Burlington" came our way in the time of Lieutenant-Governor Simcoe, who is given credit for scattering so many place names from Yorkshire around Upper Canada (York, Scarborough, Whitby, Pickering, and many more). "Burlington" is the phonetic spelling of the Yorkshire summer resort now spelled "Bridlington" but pronounced "Burlington," and formerly spelled variously as Burlington, Bridlington and Brellington. The Yorkshire Burlington, as we may call it, is a popular summer resort with a fine sandy beach and promenades, a small harbour, a bay called Burlington Bay, and a steep escarpment to the north where a great spur of rock, Flamborough Head, projects eastward. Mrs. Simcoe, writing up her diary notes from the vantage point of our beach strip in 1795, saw the Escarpment and the resemblance to that long-established Yorkshire town.

*Above: Archdeacon Spence with two
of his three thousand flags
Facing page: An avenue in Roseland*

Burlington, Ontario, has changed during the past century, just as the borough of Bridlington has altered during the nine centuries since the Norman Conquest. What will our city's future be one hundred years from now? Or even at the beginning of the next century, only five years away? We want to predict that the revitalization of our downtown, so well begun in the past year or two, will continue. Conservation of our valuable resources, both natural and cultural, will appreciate and increase. And more people will choose to move here, to live and work in Burlington. It is—as John de Visser's photographs clearly show—a remarkable place. We may share the confidence of W.D. Flatt, who declared in 1912, "We know that this district affords a most delightful place for residence," and we "have every reason to believe that we shall see our ideal realized."

The Skyway at sunset

SELECT BIBLIOGRAPHY

Balbar, George. *Burlington: Images of a City*. St. Catharines: Vanwell Publishing, 1989.

Byers, Mary, and Margaret McBurney. *The Governor's Road*. Toronto: University of Toronto Press, 1982.

Craig, Martha. *The Garden of Canada.* Toronto: William Briggs, 1902; reprinted by the Burlington Historical Society in 1967. Both editions out of print.

Emery, Claire, and Barbara Ford. *From Pathway to Skyway*. Confederation Centennial Committee of Burlington, 1967. Out of print.

Flatt, W.D. *Lakeshore Surveys,* 1912. Out of print.

———. *The Trail of Love,* 1916. Out of print.

Keough, Pat and Rosemarie. *The Niagara Escarpment: A Portfolio*. Don Mills: Stoddart, 1990.

Kelsay, Isabel Thompson. *Joseph Brant, 1743–1807: Man of Two Worlds.* Syracuse: Syracuse University Press, 1984.

Track, Norman S. *Canada's Royal Garden: Portraits and Reflections.* Toronto: Viking/Penguin Books Canada, 1994.

Turcotte, Dorothy. *The Sand Strip: Burlington/Hamilton Beaches.* St. Catharines: Stonehouse Publications, 1987.

———. *Burlington: Memories of Pioneer Days.* Erin: Boston Mills Press, 1989.

———. *Remember the Brant Inn.* Erin: Boston Mills Press, 1990.

———. *Burlington: The Growing Years.* Burlington Historical Society, 1992.

———. *Places and People on Bronte Creek.* Grimsby: Dorothy Turcotte, 1993.

*Top: Face painting
in the Burlington
Children's Festival*

*Below:
Waiting for the
Sound of Music
Festival parade,
rain or shine*